Knowing With Purpose

Your Self-Help Guide To Finding Purpose, Passion And Fulfillment

Heather Rhone

KNOWING WITH PURPOSE. Copyright © 2023. Heather Rhone. All Rights Reserved.

Printed in the United States of America.

No portion of this book may be reproduced, stored in a retrieval system, or transmitted in any form or by any means, except for brief quotations in printed reviews, without the prior written permission of DayeLight Publishers or Heather Rhone.

ISBN: 978-1-958443-45-3 (paperback)

"We are never too learned to learn."

—Heather Rhone

Acknowledgements

Thank You, God, for entrusting me with gifts so I can be of service to others as You continue to refine my qualities for Your purpose. Thank You for inspiring me to write this book and for placing the right people in my life throughout my various seasons: people who continue to positively impact my life and those who I will impact.

Thanks to my family, friends, and everyone who contributed to this book being finalized. It is my wish that this book enlightens you to the endless possibilities life has to offer while assisting you and others in navigating any challenges you may face.

Table of Contents

Acknowledgements v

Introduction 9

What Is Purpose? 11

Chapter 1: It All Begins In The Mind 13

Chapter 2: Self-Love 19

Chapter 3: Gratitude 23

Chapter 4: Life Is About Choices 27

Chapter 5: Knowing Your Season 31

Chapter 6: Knowing Your Value 35

Chapter 7: Be Selective About Your Circle 39

Chapter 8: Being Still 43

Chapter 9: Being of Service 47

Chapter 10: Knowing Who And Whose You Are 51

Chapter 11: Celebrating Others Wins As You Would Your Own 55

Chapter 12: Fulfilling Your Life's Purpose 59

Chapter 13: Isolation Leads to Transformation 63

Chapter 14: Self-Belief 67

Chapter 15: Knowing Your Purpose 71

Chapter 16: The Importance Of Goal Setting 75

Chapter 17: God Is The True Source 79

Conclusion 83

Sample Accountability Journal 85

Introduction

This travel-size book is intended to provide the reader with insightful nuggets to assist in finding and fulfilling their purpose by giving a glimpse of my journey to finding purpose through my own experience and the lessons learned along the way.

While there is no set formula to finding purpose and success, what is true is that having faith, determination, focus, self-belief, and the right people around you remain some of the critical factors in attaining the success you desire.

What Is Purpose?

Purpose refers to the reason for which something is created. It acts as an inner driving force toward achieving one's goals by incorporating the unique behaviors and skills necessary to bring that purpose to reality.

Purpose also acts as a guide towards us constantly evolving, challenging ourselves, and organizing our lives in a way that fosters true personal and spiritual growth. Living a life that honors our inner knowing and calling will ultimately lead to a feeling of empowerment and fulfillment.

Chapter 1
It All Begins In The Mind

Have you ever heard the question, "Why are you always so happy and calm like nothing bothers you?" Well, as far back as I can remember, I have always heard that. The truth is, we all go through challenges in life—good and bad—but we must be deliberate about the state we choose to remain.

So, here I was, after being in a corporate job for twenty-five years, finding myself at a crossroads and feeling unfulfilled, knowing there was more in me that I wanted to share with the world. I had a huge decision to make. It wasn't easy, but I decided to pursue purpose, and that made a world of difference.

The truth most people fail to realize is that happiness is intrinsic and it is a choice. The quality and outcome of our life is directly related to the choices we make, that is, the people we have around us, our belief system, and what we feed our minds on (print, media, etc.). Collectively, these all play a part in creating a mindset that will inevitably result in the quality of life we desire.

Knowing With Purpose

Owning your *own* reality without competing with others and without fear of rejection or disappointment is the first step toward success. True success is being at peace with the decisions you make regardless of the outcome because everything in life we experience is either a LESSON or a BLESSING.

Mindset is everything. Some of the most successful people in the world never went to college. Conversely, there are some of the more qualified individuals who are not as successful. So, what accounts for this anomaly, you may ask. Well, it all goes back to mindset.

What is your mindset? Is it a scarcity mindset? Do you believe if someone is successful, it means you won't be, or is it an abundance mindset? Do you believe there are limitless opportunities for everyone?

I didn't have a college degree when I entered the world of work at eighteen years old, but I took advantage of the opportunities provided by the company I worked for. For example, I was able to pursue certified professional programs, which enriched my performance on the job. Additionally, I attained my first home and car in my mid-twenties while being a working single mother. In my mid-forties, I decided to resign from my corporate job and focus on pursuing purpose. It took prayer, determination, the right mindset, inspiring persons around me, and the knowledge that God, our Father in heaven, is the *only* true source to propel me forward.

The truth is, some people only see the end product but are not prepared to do the groundwork to get where they want to be. Instead, they may try to discredit your genuine efforts to make themselves feel better for where they are in their lives, although presented with similar opportunities. Just keep pushing. It is therefore important to know and to surround yourself with your tribe.

Sadly, the reason for many persons' lack of true success is that there are too many "still people"—still complaining and still comparing. Stay away from "still people;" growth doesn't reside there. These are persons who spend their time looking at what others are doing while opportunities and time pass them by. The root cause of this, of course, goes back to the mindset and limitations people put on themselves and others. True success is far more. Ambition and solid qualities have far more currency in today's world, as that is what makes you truly irreplaceable because it creates your value—know it, own it. This, however, can only be developed through the right mindset.

Start today by changing the way you view life by simply adjusting your mindset. Maybe now is the time to declutter. How about reading a self-help book to elevate your mindset? Improve your prayer life to get more connected to God and assess the people around you; that is, notice those who are happy or sad for your wins. If the people around you are not building you up and encouraging you to be a better version of yourself, then find the courage to let them go and wish them well. They will only hold you back.

Knowing With Purpose

Be bold, be fierce, and don't let anyone control your life's outcome. Remember, God is the Author of our lives, if we allow Him. Don't take the pen away from Him, and you will see His perfect will for your life unfold.

Reflection

Write down one positive thing you did today.
_____
_____

Write down one positive thing you read today.
_____
_____

Write down one positive thing you shared today.
_____
_____

Write down one positive thing you watched today.
_____
_____

Write down one positive thing you said today.
_____
_____
_____
_____
_____

Chapter 2
Self-Love

Love begins with you. How often have you heard the phrase, "If you don't love yourself, you can't love anyone else." The truth is, you cannot pour into another that which you have no knowledge of. Case in point, can a dentist perform heart surgery? He is a doctor, yes, but that is not his area of expertise. He would have to study that area in order to perform heart surgery successfully. Similarly, if we have no knowledge of God, we can't know love. God gives us the spirit of love and peace as His Spirit does not dwell in noise or confusion.

Many people are always unhappy no matter what, simply because they are looking for love outside of themselves. Self-love is very important as it gives you the strength to have the confidence to walk away from people and situations that do not recognize your value and the self-respect to priortise those things that are good for both your physical and emotional well-being. Some will be baffled by the choices you make, but don't waste time explaining yourself to anyone. When the Spirit of God resides in you, you literally have no room for playing small. God equips us with what we need so that we attract the people, situations, and

Knowing With Purpose

things that are aligned to our destiny and, conversely, removes those things that are not aligned—trust Him. You will be amazed how He moves situations around to align with His will for your life.

Self-respect and self-love therefore mean that we allow ourselves to accept only those things that are deserving of our time and attention. It also means thinking of ourselves as being worthy and choosing only those things that are worthwhile. Self-love translates into the things we choose to accept for ourselves and from others. Therefore, knowing your worth is the first step in attaining self-love.

Reflection

List five ways in which you practice self-love.
_____
_____
_____
_____
_____
_____
_____

List five ways in which you express love to others.
_____
_____
_____
_____
_____
_____
_____
_____

"Thou shalt love thy neighbour as thyself. There is none other commandment greater than these." (Mark 12:31b – KJV).

Chapter 3
Gratitude

Gratitude means to give thanks for something. Arguably, the two most powerful words in life are "Thank you." "Thank you" is an acknowledgment that gives both parties a feeling of satisfaction.

Being grateful is a big deal because, believe it or not, no matter how bad you think your life is, you are still doing better than someone else. As you start to review your life, you will see that there is so much to be grateful for.

Gratitude says to the universe, "Thank you in advance for what I have already received and what is to come." Had I not been obedient to God, maybe I would not have had the opportunity to discover my ability to help others positively transform their lives. Looking back, people always came to me for advice, and I felt a sense of satisfaction at being able to guide them, not knowing what it would translate to today. When I left my job in 2021, by faith, I was able to take the time to discover my inner passions. It was amazing how God divinely provided for me during this time and, through this, I was also able to assist others. You see, being grateful, no matter how big or small, releases the same feeling of endorphins in the body that makes us feel good, and everyone likes to feel good. Don't we?

A simple yet powerful activity I have introduced to a few persons is the concept of a gratitude jar, which has yielded many positive changes with regard to their outlook on life. It is a practice I maintain myself and would encourage everyone to try. You would be amazed how much you have to be grateful for.

Sometimes we just need a reminder that it is the little things that make life so much more meaningful. So be grateful for what God does in your life—big or small—as everything He does is with purpose. It was through leaving my job that I discovered my inner passions and, through my experiences, I am now better equipped to help others.

Reflection

State one challenge you are currently facing.

_____
_____
_____
_____
_____
_____
_____
_____

What opportunity have you discovered in that challenge?

_____
_____
_____
_____
_____
_____
_____
_____
_____
_____
_____

Chapter 4
Life Is About Choices

When faced with important life decisions, you must be prepared to be in the midst of the noise and still be calm in your heart to be able to hear that inner voice and trust it.

I can remember when I was faced with the big decision to resign from my job. I went through several doubting moments as to whether or not I was making the right decision. One Friday morning, in the middle of the pandemic, having finally made up my mind, I printed a copy of my resignation letter. After all, I knew I was feeling unfulfilled, and there comes a point in each of our lives where we recognize that we want more for ourselves. It is called growth, and I was at that point.

Throughout my life, when making important life decisions, I learned to trust my inner guiding voice. I found that those were the decisions that turned out to be the ones I regretted the least because they were not made at the spur of the moment but rather out of deep reflection and thought, so whatever the outcome, I was at peace.

Needless to say, I did not hand in my letter that Friday as I was being convinced otherwise. I thought about it for the entire weekend and agonized with God. Instructively, I actually commenced writing my book that very weekend. As the ideas flowed, it was then that I knew I was ready to pursue my purpose, as through my experience, I could be an inspiration to others to go after their dreams, whatever that looks like. This was literally a light bulb moment and led to the birth of my book "**Knowing With Purpose**."

Two weeks later, I headed to the office and handed in my resignation letter. I can recall the HR Manager asking me if I was sure, considering it was in the middle of a pandemic. I was heartened by her seemingly genuine concern but just knew in my heart I had made the right decision, even though I didn't quite know what the future would quite look like yet. I took the leap of faith anyway. The truth is, when making any decision, it is never going to be the right time as there will always be something to consider. Your decisions should not be solely based on whether or not you have a backup plan; however, you should be responsible in making your important life decisions, particularly when there are other variables to be considered. Notwithstanding this, your decisions should be based on the principle that if something no longer serves or grows you, let it go. The minute you do that, the opportunities will come, and you should be ready to seize them. If they don't come, then reach within and bring them to life.

Reflection

State five things you are choosing to change to improve your life starting today.

_____
_____
_____
_____
_____
_____
_____
_____
_____
_____
_____
_____
_____
_____
_____
_____
_____
_____
_____
_____
_____
_____

Chapter 5
Knowing Your Season

It is important for us to know the season we are in and prepare for it. Are you in your sowing season or your harvest? It is very important to know so that when you begin experiencing the process, you know what it is and can act accordingly. Through constant prayer, God will reveal to you what you need to know. Sometimes your plan and His plan are not aligned. I discovered during one of my seasons that God had a different plan. He was teaching me patience and to trust His timing. Every time I decided to leave, there would literally be a delay for some reason or another. I was then convinced that it was something spiritual.

I was feeling unfulfilled, and by this time, the work environment had become very unhealthy. I decided to be obedient and remain still, and in that stillness, so much was revealed to me about the people around me. I discovered the naysayers, the enablers, and the supporters. God was revealing to me those things I needed to know. It was during my alone time however that I got the greatest clarity. God was paving the way for me to discern those things that were not aligned with my destiny. God's timing is perfect, and we must learn to trust it.

Knowing With Purpose

Every conversation I had during that season was important; every experience, every action, and subsequent reaction was important. I was learning more about myself and the people around me, and I am grateful for the persons God placed in my life who assisted me in navigating that season.

You should never feel guilty for setting healthy boundaries; neither should you accept persons trying to project parts of themselves that they dislike unto you. The minute you identify these unhealthy behaviours, speak your truth, and remove yourself as soon as you can so as not to allow yourself to be a means through which these unhealthy persons try to regulate their emotions. I have found that persons who are threatened by your accomplishments tend to be quite focused on you and will try to destroy or sabotage you. Don't worry; others will eventually see through it like you did.

Collectively, however, when we choose to operate from a place of love, we will not be easily manipulated by persons who operate from a place of fear, so be discerning and maintain your inner peace and happiness regardless.

It is a fact therefore that when you are authentic, unhealthy individuals may try to destroy everything that is beautiful about you because, at their core, they truly lack those qualities within themselves. So, honour your authenticity by staying true to who you are, knowing there can only be one you. The ones who truly know you will see through it, and the ones who have a true desire to grow will be inspired.

Either way, adversity presents a good opportunity for you to know your people, as it is during those times that the truth is revealed.

I can recall a conversation I had during that season. That encounter led to me feeling empowered to pen my book as I saw this as an opportunity that could help others. I came up with the headings for the chapters that day, and although I didn't start to pen the content, it was the start of something. I wrote the first few chapters that very weekend, and I knew God had a plan.

Sometimes, for our own well-being, we have to be willing to quickly assess and let go of certain situations that no longer contribute to our growth. We must understand that we are all at different levels on our life's journey, so this assessment becomes necessary at times to allow persons to become accountable so they too can do the inner work and self-reflection necessary in becoming more robust individuals.

Let us therefore use our experiences to propel us into our purpose so that we can help ignite the change we want to see in the world.

Reflection

Do you know the season you are in right now? If yes, state it here.

_____

_____

_____

_____

_____

_____

_____

List the lessons and/or blessings you received in your season.

_____

_____

_____

_____

_____

_____

_____

_____

_____

_____

_____

Chapter 6
Knowing Your Value

Your value should not be determined by the voices around you but rather by your inner guiding voice. Your Father in heaven chose you, therefore, you are a rare gem and should be treated as such. When you undervalue yourself, you give permission to the world to undervalue who you are. You must be able to stand in your truth as a human being and recognize that you are in control of your destiny. Once you allow yourself to stay connected to God, He will reveal His purpose to you, and you will literally see Him move things in accordance with His direction for your life; therefore, don't be afraid to let go of those things that are not aligned to your destiny.

Too many of us turn a blind eye and find excuses for abusive behaviors and people's lack of respect for our boundaries. It is a fact that when people show you who they are, believe them the first time. Otherwise, you will keep repeating the same cycles, causing you to lose your self-worth and value.

The less emphasis you place on the opinions of others, the more successful you will be. Remember that judgments are a mere admission of one's own character. On a subconscious level, we see people not necessarily as they are but as we ourselves are. So, don't take it personally. It has nothing to do with you, but rather understand that they are persons who are fighting their own internal battles. When they can't control you, they will try to control how others view you, so just pray for them and release it.

Finally, healthy situations will always provide the space, opportunity, and autonomy for you to grow and choose what is best for you. Therefore, never compromise yourself, your goals, or dreams for anything. Be grateful for where you are thus far on your journey, and for the help you gave and received along the way. Pay it forward, but never allow yourself to be a slave to anything. Keep moving forward and always recognize your value. Therefore, once you know what you don't want or won't accept, then the rest will fall into place. We signal to others how we want to be treated by what we accept and what we continue to allow.

Reflection

How do you see yourself?

_____
_____
_____
_____
_____
_____

List three ways in which you show that you value yourself.

_____
_____
_____
_____
_____

List three ways in which you show that you value others.

_____
_____
_____
_____
_____

Chapter 7
Be Selective About Your Circle

In the same way what you feed your mind with affects the quality of your life, so does who you choose to surround yourself with. Keep in mind, it is less important to have a lot of people around you and more important to have a few quality people around you—choose the latter. Authentic people tend to have less people around them for that very reason. The persons you choose to keep the closest to you should be persons who will celebrate your wins, are there for your losses, and will allow you room to grow. These are questions you should answer in relation to your inner circle: "How do they react in my low moments? How do they react in my high moments?" If you pay attention, you will know your people.

Along my journey, I have always found myself around persons who were higher achievers than myself, and what I found is that this inspired me to be the best version of myself. It is important to surround yourself with people who can impact your life positively, those who you can learn from and vice versa.

Knowing With Purpose

We are truly what we think about most and, for that reason, I am very deliberate about the energies I allow in my space, whether it be people, media, etc. Not everyone should have access to you. It may not make you the most popular, but you will have peace of mind and less drama in your life.

Whenever you are on a certain life path, particularly when you are spiritually connected, it is very important to recognize the people who are aligned with your destiny and those who aren't, and act accordingly, as this can either make or break you. It is therefore very important to seek wisdom in discerning those around you to determine whether they are there to distract, destroy, or help you fulfil your purpose.

It is also important to see everyone as being a human being first, regardless of their abilities or position in life. The minute we start seeing people as greater than or less than ourselves, we begin to develop inferiority complexes, and that can lead to a plethora of unhealthy behaviors. Being able to relate to people at all levels without the desire to be in competition speaks to being very secure in who you are as a person and can only aid in you becoming who are meant to be in this life. The notion of not feeling less than regardless of is, to me, truly one of the biggest gifts you can give yourself.

Reflection

Name three qualities you look for in a friend.

_____

_____

_____

_____

_____

_____

Do you possess any of those qualities?

_____

_____

_____

_____

_____

_____

If no, work on being those three things to a friend in the next thirty days. Ask for feedback and write it here!

_____

_____

_____

_____

Chapter 8
Being Still

Most of us have this habit of pre-empting the next word someone is going to say, either because they are taking too long to get to the point or it could be that we just think we know it all. I am guilty of that sometimes, but we are never too learned to learn, and nothing trumps experience. It is important however to become so self-aware that we are able to catch ourselves in those moments and make the necessary adjustments. Learning the art of active listening and stillness gives us a chance to gain a better understanding of whatever situation we may face.

It is a fact that not everyone should be allowed to speak into our lives, but certainly there are those persons whose opinions we regard, and therefore we should allow ourselves the humility to say, "I don't know everything. What do you think?" Sometimes those persons may be able to look at things from a different perspective than ours. By using our discernment, this can help guide us to better decision-making, as well as allow us to learn from each other. Ultimately, however, it is important to place all our final decisions before God, as He always knows what is best for us.

Therefore, taking the time to listen not only allows us to process things on a deeper level but also to gain clarity. I have personally benefited from just allowing myself to listen and not respond. This process allows us to make better decisions as they are not based solely on emotions. Further, it is usually in those moments of stillness that God speaks to us. Have you ever heard of the term "Gut feeling?" Yes, it is that feeling you get deep inside, and it is God's way of guiding us toward a particular decision, but we must learn to be still in those moments and ask for God's guidance in helping us to discern His voice.

Finally, if your decision brings you peace and closer to God, then you have made the right decision.

Reflection

List three things you are passionate about.

_____
_____
_____
_____
_____
_____
_____
_____
_____
_____
_____
_____
_____
_____
_____
_____
_____
_____

Take some time to just be still and connect with God. Ask Him to help reveal your gift/s.

Chapter 9
Being of Service

The whole point of us being on this earth is to be of service to others and to get others to know God. The ultimate feeling of fulfillment is that of feeling you have made an impact and a difference. Whatever that looks like is inevitably up to you through the guidance of the Holy Spirit.

When I resigned from my job, I knew I had to do something I was passionate about. I also knew I was at a point in my career where I believed I had so much more to offer. I was determined not to allow anything to distract me from that, and I just knew it was the right time.

One of the reasons I decided to write this book was along the lines of being of service. Throughout the last few years of my journey, I witnessed a lot of persons in dire need of a mindset purge. I got the inspiration but needed the right environment to gain clarity in order to translate that into something of value. In my solitude, I was able to do just that, which underscored the value of alone time.

Knowing With Purpose

It is important that we recognize that the world represents abundance and there is enough for everyone. Moreover, it is important to always see yourself as ENOUGH because negative attitudes only lead to negative results. Furthermore, the quality of your life is an external manifestation of your own mindset. So, honor yourself by being true to who you really are and don't waste your life trying to live someone else's or you will become resentful when you don't get the same results as no two persons are the same. Most importantly, allow yourself time to truly heal those parts of yourself that resonate with unhealed persons so that you can offer your best self to whatever situation you are placed in and you can set healthy boundaries. You are allowed to give yourself the time and space to do that.

We are all unique beings made according to God's purpose for our lives, but it is up to us to do our part in fulfilling that purpose.

Reflection

List three things you've done to make someone's life better.

_____
_____
_____
_____
_____
_____
_____
_____
_____

List three things you could do to make someone's life better in the next thirty days.

_____
_____
_____
_____
_____
_____
_____

Chapter 10
Knowing Who And Whose You Are

The word "knowing" refers to the act of doing something in full awareness or consciousness. Therefore, knowing who and whose you are is important because it guides the very core of your being. Being a Christian doesn't mean we are not human, but what it does mean is that when we fall, we have a Father who is forgiving, who loves us, and only wants the best for us, as long as we ask Him through sincere prayer and a willingness to become the best version of ourselves. Our identity is therefore found in God, not man—don't ever forget that. Having this knowledge allows us to be less tolerant in accepting projections from others; therefore, it is important to know who you are. Although life is about continuous improvement, it is equally important that you remain true to your authentic self because that is where your true value resides.

When we know how God operates in our lives, things get much simpler. It is also important to note that, as humans, we are limited in our ability to be all-knowing, so we must rely on our ability to discern God's voice to guide us in the right direction. To receive God's blessings however, we must know when to trust God so even when the way seems unclear to the human eyes, we still know that He loves us unconditionally and only wants the best for us. Sometimes that belief will require us to make some tough decisions. Even when things don't go how we expect, we can be sure that we are still on the right path.

We may miss what God is doing in our lives simply because we sometimes allow ourselves to become distracted. It is therefore important that we learn to keep focused, accept things for what they are, and keep moving forward. The truth is, sometimes all that is required is a course-correct.

Reflection

List three ways God has shown up for you.

Chapter 11
Celebrating Others Wins As You Would Your Own

There is something simply beautiful about people who genuinely love seeing others succeed.

I, personally, have always genuinely loved seeing others succeed. Seeing others grow and thrive makes me feel good inside because I know what it feels like to succeed at something, and I want others to experience that feeling. It makes me feel empowered and fulfilled.

Seeing others thriving only pushes me to want to do better for myself as it acts as a motivation, so I would always be the first to congratulate someone on their wins, be it a promotion, a new job venture or just about anything that makes their life better. It truly makes me feel good, almost as though it were me. So, I could never understand people who are sad at others' successes. It has always been mind-boggling to me, but then I remembered the old adage, "Misery loves company."

Knowing With Purpose

I can recall a friend/mentor and successful entrepreneur once told me that eagles can't hang around with sheep. Once I understood that principle, it all made sense. In order to be successful, you have to surround yourself with like-minded people who will lift you up and not try to drag you down. Life gets a bit easier once you understand this. The people you spend most of your time with will ultimately affect the trajectory of your life, so choose wisely how you spend your time.

Successful people are winners because of their mindset. Try as you might, if you don't have the right mindset, you will never truly be successful, so work on that daily. Knowing who you are—your strengths, weaknesses, people, goals—and having self-discipline, accountability, and being honest are just a few of the traits that guarantee success.

The truth is, it is not even so much about networking. That's good, but just having a conversation with the right person at the right time can yield the same result and change your life for the better. It is so important to surround yourself with people who are aligned with your destiny. It is also equally important to do a life audit from time to time, as it helps guide you toward knowing who your people are—cherish them.

Reflection

List three people in your life who you know are genuinely happy when you succeed.

Chapter 12
Fulfilling Your Life's Purpose

What are we really here for?

At the end of the day, this is what it is all about. On the last day of my job, while I was saying my final goodbyes, I recall persons saying, "Better opportunity," "More money" and so on. Reasonable thinking, I guess, but it was right then that I realized that most people are so consumed with materialism and limited beliefs, that those are the only things that seem to come to mind when someone decides to open a new chapter. The truth is, peace, happiness, growth, fulfillment, and the freedom to choose are the new wealth, as the absence of these with all the material wealth in the world is of no use.

Therefore, it is important to prioritize your well-being. Don't just live your life working to pay bills; spend some time to appreciate nature, spend time with family and loved ones, and prioritize self-care (spiritual and physical). If you are not happy about something, make a decision either way and always choose what is best for you mentally, spiritually, and emotionally, and don't apologize for it. Start a business; fulfill your dreams before you get old, so you don't get

Knowing With Purpose

consumed with regret, saying you wish you had taken that chance when you were younger. Above all, always keep God in the midst.

As we get older, we have a greater appreciation for the important things in our lives, so live below your means so you can enjoy life; travel the world if you can—it is yours to experience. Touch some lives in whatever way you can. Help those less fortunate than yourself in whatever way you can, and don't talk about it. Always be a good person, but don't waste your time proving it to anyone. Also, never let the actions of others change who you are at the core.

Trust God to direct your life's path, and enjoy the journey. Embrace the good and bad and see each as an opportunity to become a better version of yourself. Most of all, allow yourself the space to truly evolve as a person without feeling the need to explain yourself to anyone. Let them create their own narratives—that's not your problem. Most importantly, find your gift so you can be fruitful and productive.

Reflection

What is your gift?
_____
_____
_____
_____
_____
_____
_____
_____

How can you positively impact others through your gift?
_____
_____
_____
_____
_____
_____
_____
_____
_____

Chapter 13
Isolation Leads to Transformation

During my period of isolation, I decided to publicly recommit my life to God in response to His call. I became actively involved in church and served in various capacities. As I grew spiritually, it became clearer that spirituality and religion are two totally different things. Religion comes with a set of beliefs and rules that are manmade; spirituality is more about seeking a deeper spiritual connection with God on a personal level. This is what we all should seek to be; spiritual and not just religious.

We have our individual life paths and, just as the church leaders are carrying out their life's purpose, persons should not be content with just going to church and receiving the messages through sermons, but rather use that as an opportunity to look within, find their purpose and bring it to life. Remember, we were all made for a specific purpose no matter how great or small that purpose is—it matters.

For me, this journey was a bit different. I was now making decisions consciously; I was seeing things through a totally different lens. Let us not fool ourselves; the church is filled with persons who were once a part of the world, so you will find that each person's actions are directly in line with their level of spiritual growth. We must understand that so as not to become distracted. Stay focused and understand that while going to church, paying our tithes, etc. are important, ultimately, there are two main things that God truly requires of us as believers, and that is a personal relationship with Him—which includes obedience to His law—and true service to others. My true transformation came the moment I realized this because once we truly seek God, we will never be disappointed as He knows our hearts. So, understand that everyone's journey and purpose is different, and not everyone is going to understand yours, and that is fine. Therefore, don't be envious when you see God doing good things for others—you never saw their valley—your time will come.

Know that if God can make a way for someone else, He can do it for you too. Just work on your relationship with Him so you can have a testimony. He knows us by name, and once you choose Him, you will always be victorious—God can use anybody He sees fit.

As believers, we should know that sometimes when the enemy attacks, it is because there is something special God has placed inside of you, so just go within and bring that gift/s to life—the world needs it.

Embrace the future and use every experience as an opportunity to truly grow and be an inspiration to others. Remember, nothing can stop God's purpose in your life.

There may be delays and distractions, but God's purpose will always be fulfilled once you allow the Holy Spirit to guide you. He will do His work through you once you allow Him.

Reflection

What did you discover or learn about yourself during your period of isolation? How has that knowledge assisted with your growth in any area of your life?

_____
_____
_____
_____
_____
_____
_____
_____
_____
_____
_____
_____
_____
_____
_____
_____
_____
_____
_____

Chapter 14
Self-Belief

Believing in yourself is very important. It gives you the drive to go after your goals and dreams with or without the support of others. Therefore, you must know what you want out of life and forge your own path, whatever that looks like to you.

Self-belief is that inner knowing that you can make it regardless of not seeing the clear path at the beginning. The truth is, God never tests us beyond our capacity. If you desire to find purpose, believe that you have it within you to achieve whatever your mind imagines regardless of the obstacles that you may face.

Like faith, which is the belief in the unseen, self-belief requires a goal and tunnel vision. There are many great leaders who will tell you they had to fail a few times to get it right, so you and I are no different. So, while everyone's journey is different, there is one thing that remains constant, and that is the ability to believe in yourself, and that will keep you going. You have to build that kind of mindset that says, "Regardless of, I know I can achieve whatever I put my mind to once it's God's will." So, never put limitations on yourself because of others, your current situation, or procrastination. You are made for so much more. Reach and keep reaching; you will be surprised to discover the gifts you never knew you had, and when you find them, put them to good use.

It is good to have people around you to support you. Be grateful for those who do, but there are times when you have to become your biggest cheerleader in the midst of it all. Finding your purpose will require you to be prepared to close out the noise and focus. Realizing your hidden potential is truly a gift as not everyone is bold enough to pursue it, make it a reality, and use it to help in improving not only their lives but also the world around us. Therefore, for those who dare, I celebrate you. For those who want to, I say go for it.

Self-belief is simply knowing and believing on a deeper level that you can and will achieve regardless, so believe in yourself. You are a winner!

Reflection

Write down three ways that you can bolster your belief system.

_____
_____
_____
_____
_____
_____
_____
_____
_____
_____
_____
_____
_____
_____
_____
_____
_____

"I can do all things through Christ which strengthenth me." (Philippians 4:13 – KJV).

Chapter 15
Knowing Your Purpose

Sometimes it can be a daunting task to figure out your purpose. While we understand that we can have many passions and it is through those passions that we can birth our purpose, the truth is that work is meant to be enjoyed, so with the right attitude, we will be able to explore what we truly love to do. Here are a few ways to assist in breaking through your limited self-beliefs to assist in discovering your true purpose.

Give Yourself Space

Allowing yourself the space to explore those things you are passionate about is an important step in knowing your purpose. Be deliberate about exploring different areas that you are passionate about, and that will energize you; therefore, you will find it easier to identify those things that don't give you energy. As you pursue what you love, those options that you discover will eventually lead you to your life's purpose. With this in mind, you must be prepared to explore new areas that you have never considered before.

Pay Attention To Details

Sometimes our passions change as we grow. For example, although I loved being an admin for many years, my passion faded towards the end and, of course, there were many reasons for this. Notwithstanding this, however, it is not unusual for persons to have many passions, some of which they just never paid enough attention to. Somehow, as it was in my case, being a good writer was hidden in my job as an admin as I had to prepare minutes and reports on occasions. Today, I am able to be an author by utilizing those skills.

In addition, I was also able to strengthen my coaching and public speaking skills through my roles in church and other activities. None of these areas were anything I had even thought of doing as a profession but realised that they now come naturally for me. This underscores the importance of paying attention to what you are currently doing and, by so doing, you can discover your unrealized passions and seek to strengthen them.

Be Honest With Yourself

Being honest with yourself allows you to figure out what you are most passionate about. Therefore, it is important that you allow yourself to develop and engage in those passions by being willing to let go of those things that do not support that. Here are a few questions you can ask yourself to help guide the process:

i. When do I feel most energized and connected with my true self?

ii. What would I choose to do with my time, even if I weren't being paid?

iii. What skills/talents do I possess that I want to develop further to share with the world?

iv. What kind of legacy do I want to leave behind?

The Litmus Test

Always ensure that whatever you choose to do, it is something you truly want to do. It may require you to take certain courses to ensure that you are not only knowledgeable in that area but also to figure out if it is an area you actually enjoy. This will allow you to see if you have found an area that will give you long-term fulfillment.

Lastly, and most importantly, having found your passion, seek God's guidance and be very deliberate about creating a legacy that will still be useful in years to come.

Reflection

List three things you are most passionate about.

_____

_____

_____

_____

_____

_____

_____

_____

_____

Of those three things, which makes you feel most energized and fulfilled? And why?

_____

_____

_____

_____

_____

_____

_____

Chapter 16
The Importance Of Goal Setting

Goals are integral to awaken our purpose and assist us in finding true success. It is our goals that drive us to focus our attention in a way that allows us to operate with the end in mind. Therefore, goal setting requires, among other things, the right elements in order to be truly effective.

Some elements of goal setting that you will find useful are:

- Making a decision regarding the length of time and effort you are willing to endure on a particular goal in the face of genuine challenges.

- Setting realistic short and long-term goals. Also ensure that you possess the required strategy and skillsets needed in order for you to accomplish those goals.

- Employing strategies such as core self-belief and the ability to properly prioritize. These are crucial elements to goal setting as it creates a synergy that assists in creating the required outcomes.

- Getting feedback is also important. This allows us to ascertain whether or not our goals are in keeping with what we intend to achieve, and it also creates the space for us to make the necessary changes so we remain on track.

Taking charge of our goals is therefore important in finding purpose. Our overall behaviour towards life is a direct result of our choices. Further, it allows us to master our own reality, regardless of external factors, leading us to live a more meaningful life. It is also important to set goals that provide some challenge so that we are able to review our current interests relative to our previous ones and take the necessary next steps. As we continue to achieve our milestones, we will undoubtedly begin to feel more fulfilled and be well on our way to finding and fulfilling our purpose.

Reflection

List three goals you wish to achieve within the next two years. And what steps you plan to take to achieve them.

_____
_____
_____
_____
_____
_____
_____
_____
_____
_____
_____
_____
_____
_____
_____
_____
_____
_____
_____
_____
_____
_____
_____

Chapter 17
God Is The True Source

We are all made in the image and likeness of God. Let us therefore reflect His character in all we do. Like a child, when we get into adulthood, we should put away childish things. Similarly, as we grow and mature spiritually, we should also shed those things that are not of God. Of course, because we are human, we understand that everything is a process, and each of us mature at a different level spiritually and emotionally. However, we should know that God is the true source, and everything we have comes from Him. He has entrusted us with our gifts, talents, and resources as He sees fit so that we can honor Him through service to others.

We should recognize that all good gifts come from God; however, we have to be discerning. I have personally experienced God's divine provision in my life during my period of solitude: my bills were paid, I ate well, I was able to be of service, and I experienced numerous other blessings in that season, none of which I took for granted. God was teaching me in that season to rely solely on Him. You see, when you put in the work and put your trust in God, there is nothing anyone can do when He wants to bless you. When you operate with pure intentions, God will always turn things in your favour. However, He may not give you what you think you want, but you will get all that you need because He is the true source.

So, rise up and let us do our part by becoming co-creators with Source in making the world a better place, knowing that all we need is already within us.

Reflection

In what ways can you use your gifts/talents/resources to positively contribute to the world?

_____
_____
_____
_____
_____
_____
_____
_____
_____
_____
_____
_____
_____
_____
_____
_____
_____
_____
_____
_____
_____

Conclusion

I hope by now you are feeling energized and empowered to get up and take control of your own life. The time is NOW! True freedom comes from being unafraid to face new challenges and new opportunities head-on without the negative self-talk. Even if you fail, get up and try again. Be gentle and at peace with yourself for not always getting it right the first time, knowing the next time you will be operating from a position of knowledge, and nothing trumps that.

I am Heather Rhone. I am a mother, daughter, self-help author, and certified life coach, and it is a pleasure to meet you!

"The meaning of life is to **find your gift;** the **purpose of life** is to **give it away.**" —**Pablo Picasso**

Rise up, winners!

Thank You...

...to my readers for joining me on this journey. It is my hope that this book will assist you in improving your lives and be an inspiration to you and your families to be bold enough to pursue your purpose and dreams no matter the obstacles you may face.

If this book has been an inspiration to you, please feel free to spread the word and leave a review so that others may also share in the experience.

I may be reached at heatherrhone1@gmail.com

I wish you love, peace, and blessings always.

—Heather

Sample Accountability Journal

(Replicate this weekly, monthly, or annually, depending on your goals).

One week passion/goal/purpose finder.

Day 1

What small action can you take toward moving toward your goal/passion/purpose?

_____
_____
_____
_____
_____
_____
_____
_____
_____
_____
_____
_____
_____
_____
_____
_____
_____
_____
_____
_____
_____

Day 2

What is hindering you from pursuing your goal? How can you overcome it?

_____
_____
_____
_____
_____
_____
_____
_____
_____
_____
_____
_____
_____
_____
_____
_____
_____
_____
_____
_____
_____

Day 3

List the things you are passionate about.

Day 4

How can you work on refining those things that you are passionate about?

_____

Day 5

What are the ways in which you can turn your passion into purpose using your gift/s?

Day 6

What are the things that you are prepared to give up to achieve your purpose? What help will you need on this journey?

Day 7

What passion /goal/purpose have you decided to pursue (State time-frame, for example: In the next six months, one year, etc.)

_____
_____
_____
_____
_____
_____
_____
_____
_____
_____
_____
_____
_____
_____
_____
_____
_____
_____
_____
_____
_____

Notes

Notes

www.ingramcontent.com/pod-product-compliance
Lightning Source LLC
Chambersburg PA
CBHW070323100426
42743CB00011B/2533